SUPER TECH
SPACE

CLIVE GIFFORD • CHELEN ÉCIJA

WAYLAND

First published in Great Britain in 2024
by Wayland
Copyright © Hodder and Stoughton, 2024
All rights reserved

Editors: Elise Short, Jenni Lazell
Designer: Lisa Peacock

HB ISBN: 978 1 5263 2575 4
PB ISBN: 978 1 5263 2576 1

Printed and bound in Dubai

Wayland, an imprint of
Hachette Children's Group
Part of Hodder and Stoughton
Carmelite House
50 Victoria Embankment
London EC4Y 0DZ
An Hachette UK Company
www.hachette.co.uk
www.hachettechildrens.co.uk

CONTENTS

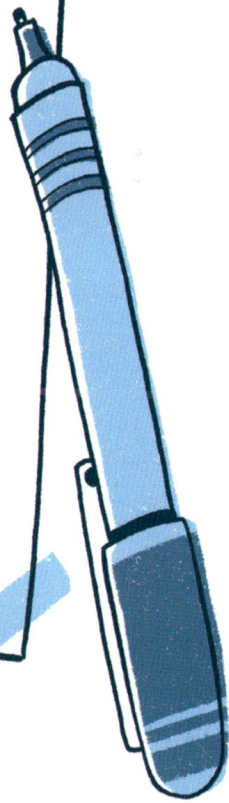

INTRODUCTION

Space has fascinated people for thousands of years. It was only in the 1950s, though, that the tech was developed to first launch machines and, later, people above Earth to go and explore the Universe.

In 1957, Sputnik became the first machine to orbit Earth. Four years later, Yuri Gagarin became the first man in space followed by the first woman, Valentina Tereshkova, in 1963.

Since that time, people have voyaged to and stood on the Moon, lived for months at a time in space stations orbiting Earth and sent robotic probes to explore all the other planets in our solar system.

OSIRIS-REx has already landed on one asteroid and is off hunting another one which it will reach in 2029. The probe gathers samples from each asteroid and sends them back on long journeys to Earth.

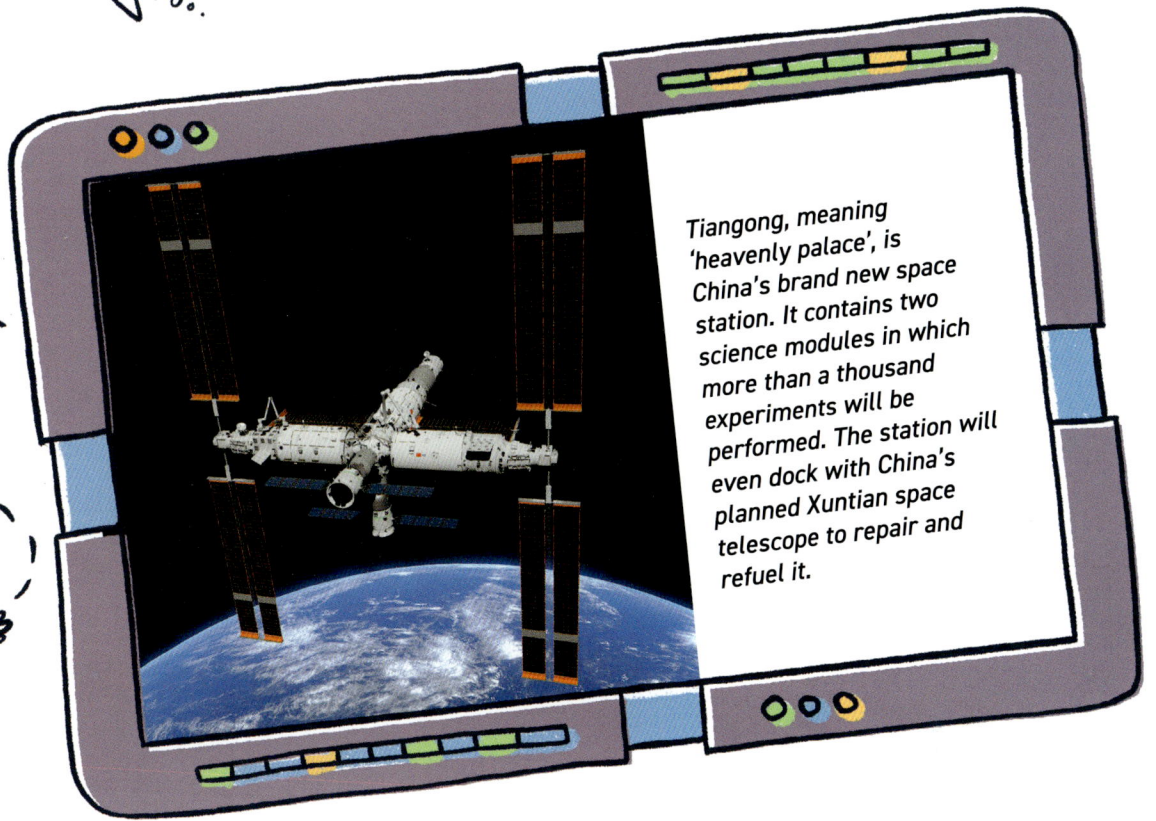

Tiangong, meaning 'heavenly palace', is China's brand new space station. It contains two science modules in which more than a thousand experiments will be performed. The station will even dock with China's planned Xuntian space telescope to repair and refuel it.

Space tech continues to evolve and advance and the future looks extremely exciting ...

It is likely that humans will return to the Moon and, if they do, they may explore in exciting new electric rovers such as this Japanese six-wheeler.

POWERING THROUGH SPACE

SPACEX STARSHIP

Most spacecraft use rocket engines to power them through space. Starship is launched by a Super Heavy launch vehicle which contains 33 rocket engines that burn fuel and oxygen. Once this is used up, Super Heavy falls away and Starship's own rocket engines fire to carry it higher.

SPACESHIP III

Virgin Galactic's spaceplane will be launched high in the sky, slung underneath a carrier aircraft. At 15,000 m above ground, SpaceShip III will be released, its rocket engines will fire and it will head into space, carrying six passengers on a short space voyage before landing on the ground like a regular aircraft.

LIGHTSAIL 2

Crowdfunded by the public, this unusual space probe orbited 720 km above Earth. It was powered not by a rocket engine but by particles of light from the Sun. These gently pushed its large, square sail, giving it slow but fuel-free travel through space as it took photos of Earth.

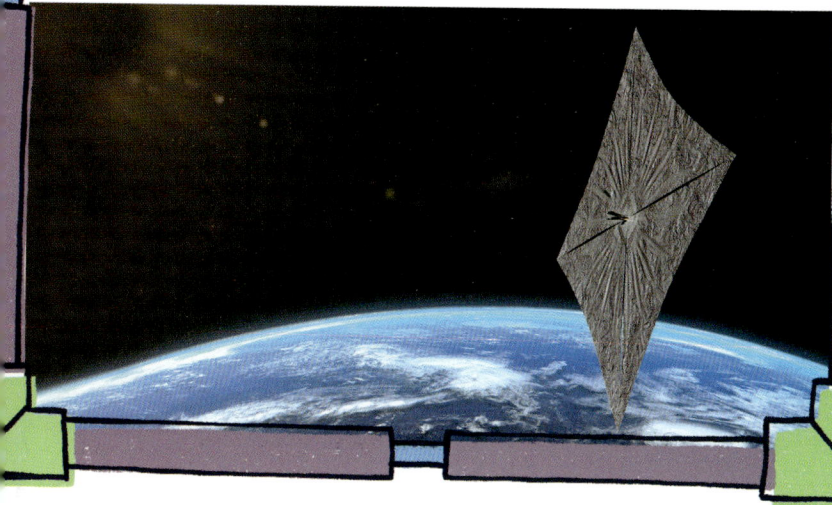

Send me those sweet light particles, Sun!

Round and round the Moon I go.

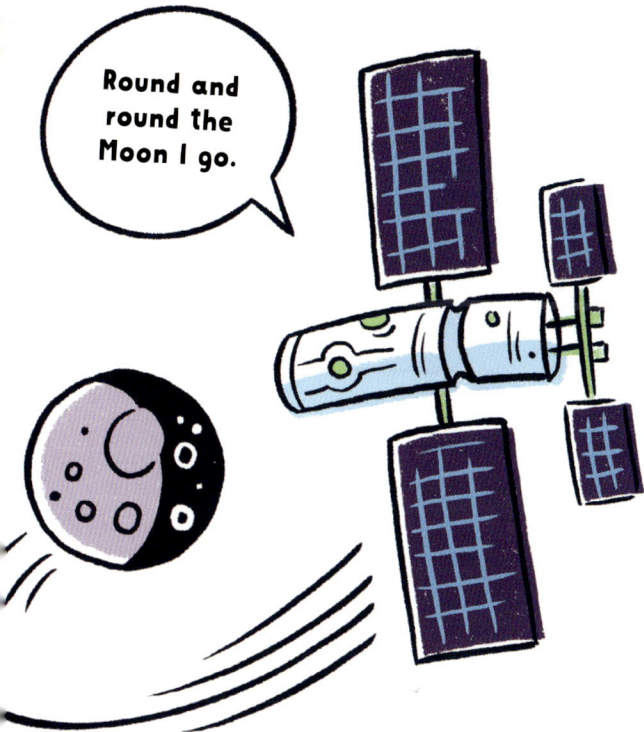

LUNAR GATEWAY

NASA's exciting new space station may orbit the Moon in the late 2020s and 2030s. It would get there without using rocket engines. Instead, gigantic solar panels would generate enough electricity to power its electric ion engines, which would thrust the craft through space.

A CLOSER LOOK AT:
THE SPACE LAUNCH SYSTEM

Space rockets have a weight problem. The heavier they are, the more power they need to get off the ground and into space. Bigger engines and more fuel mean even more weight. The solution is to build multi-stage rockets like NASA's new Space Launch System, or SLS for short.

The four giant rocket engines in SLS's first stage all fire up. Powerful pumps mix fuel and liquid oxygen together in the combustion chamber. The mixture is set alight and burns fiercely.

At launch, the whole SLS weighs 2.6 million kg – about the weight of 440 African elephants. That's heavy!

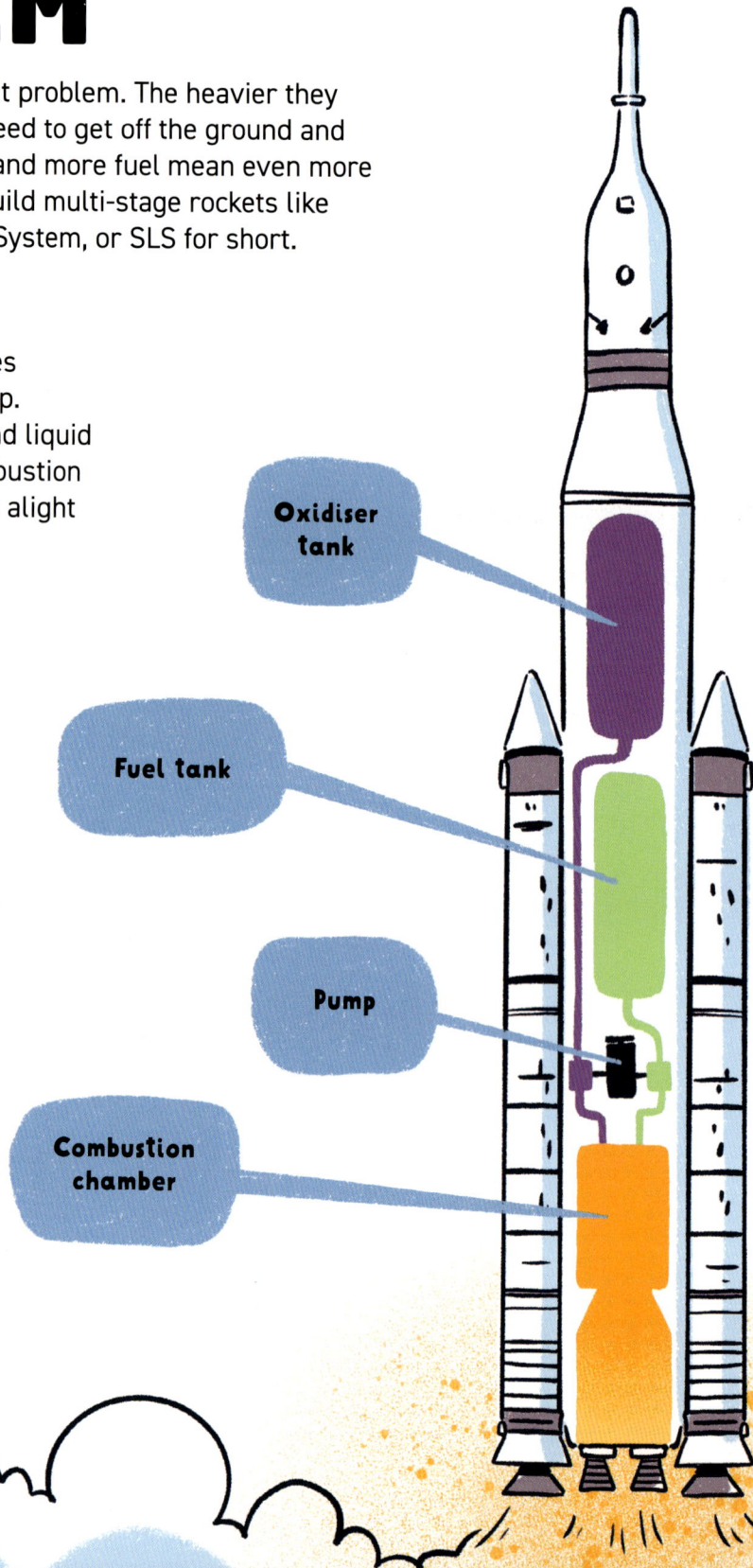

Oxidiser tank

Fuel tank

Pump

Combustion chamber

As the mixture burns, it creates rapidly expanding gases which thrust out of the engines' exhaust. The gases create a force in the opposite direction, propelling the rocket into the air.

Each of the SLS's two booster rockets, which create extra power, are as tall as a 17-storey building.

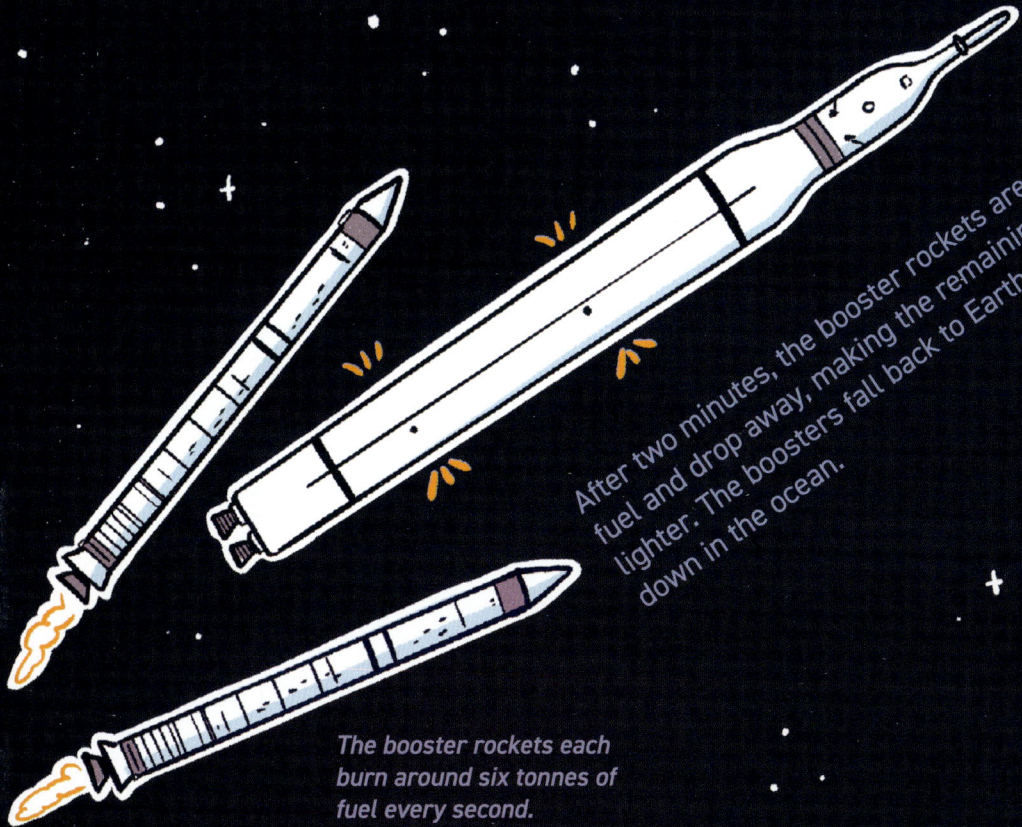

After two minutes, the booster rockets are out of fuel and drop away, making the remaining rocket lighter. The boosters fall back to Earth, splashing down in the ocean.

The booster rockets each burn around six tonnes of fuel every second.

After eight minutes or so, the first stage's rocket engines have burned up all their fuel and the rocket is around 160 km above Earth. Explosive bolts fire and the first stage separates from the rest of the rocket, removing lots of no-longer needed weight.

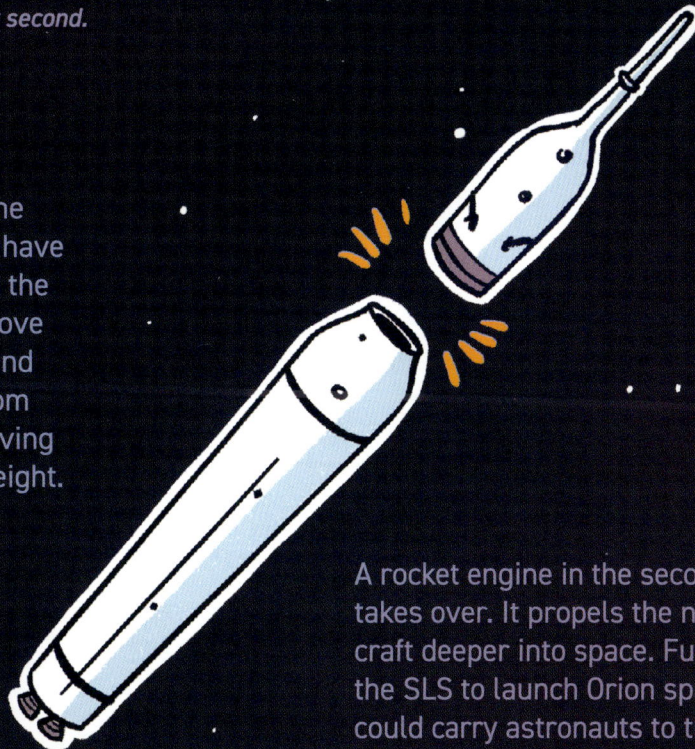

A rocket engine in the second stage now takes over. It propels the now much lighter craft deeper into space. Future plans are for the SLS to launch Orion spacecraft which could carry astronauts to the Moon.

SENSING SPACE

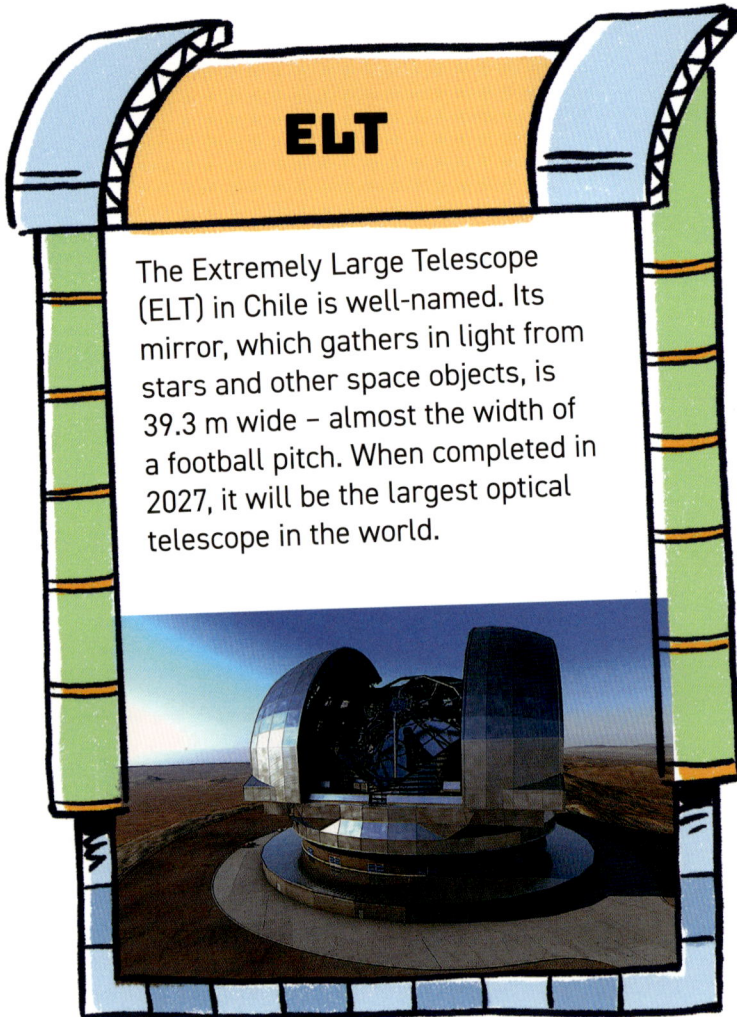

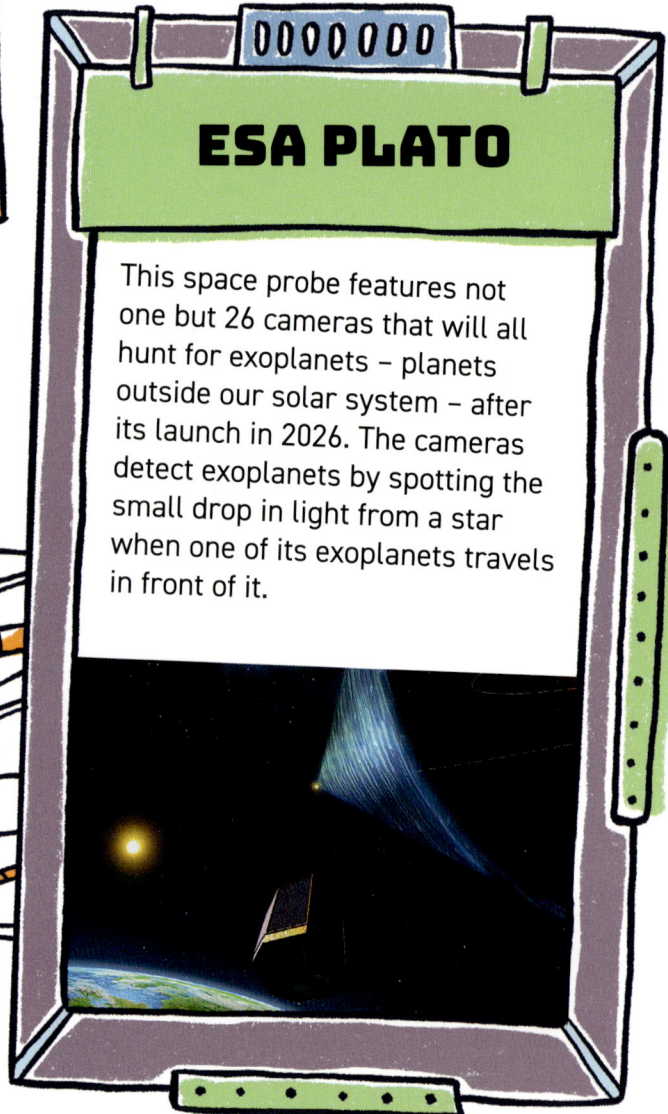

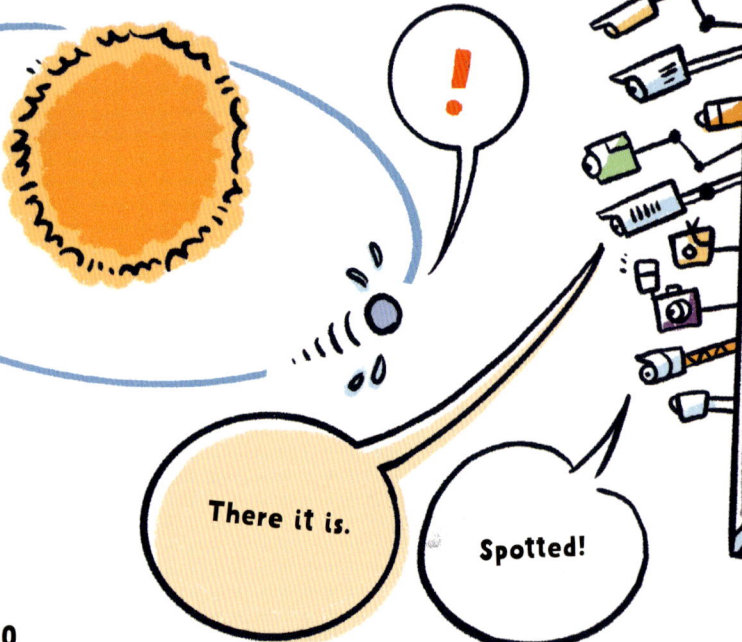

ELT

The Extremely Large Telescope (ELT) in Chile is well-named. Its mirror, which gathers in light from stars and other space objects, is 39.3 m wide – almost the width of a football pitch. When completed in 2027, it will be the largest optical telescope in the world.

ESA PLATO

This space probe features not one but 26 cameras that will all hunt for exoplanets – planets outside our solar system – after its launch in 2026. The cameras detect exoplanets by spotting the small drop in light from a star when one of its exoplanets travels in front of it.

!

There it is.

Spotted!

FAST

Radio telescopes gather in radio waves from space to build up pictures of distant galaxies. The bigger the radio dish, the more distant the signals it can capture. China's FAST radio dish is the world's largest. It is 500 m wide and made up of 4,500 panels.

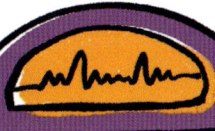

THE NANCY GRACE ROMAN SPACE TELESCOPE

Named after a famous female astronomer, this telescope will blast off into space in 2027 and, over its five year mission, measure the light from one billion galaxies. It will also gather infrared heat energy given off by exoplanets to measure them.

THE JAMES WEBB SPACE TELESCOPE

This American telescope, known as the JWST, is the successor to the world famous Hubble Space Telescope. The JWST was launched on Christmas Day, 2021 and operates 1.5 million km away from Earth.

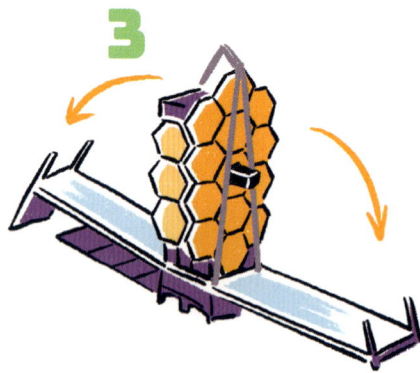

It's nice to stretch out.

This telescope was launched crammed inside the top of an Ariane 6 rocket. Once in space, it slowly unfolded its giant mirror and sun shield in stages over a period of 12 days.

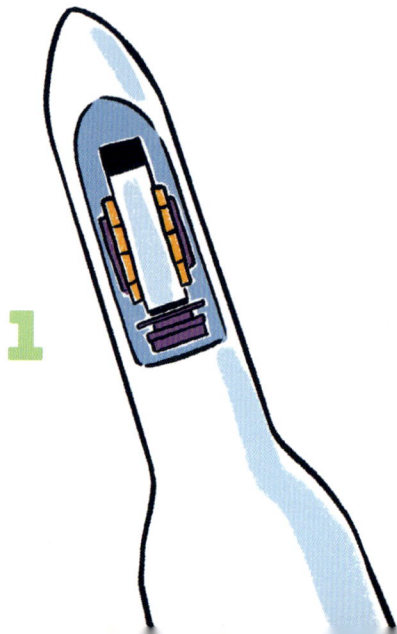

I stand 6.5 m tall and am made of 18 six-sided panels each coated in pure gold to reflect light well.

The JWST's mirror gathers in seven times more light than the Hubble's mirror. It is so powerful it can detect objects in space that shine 400 times more faintly than other telescopes.

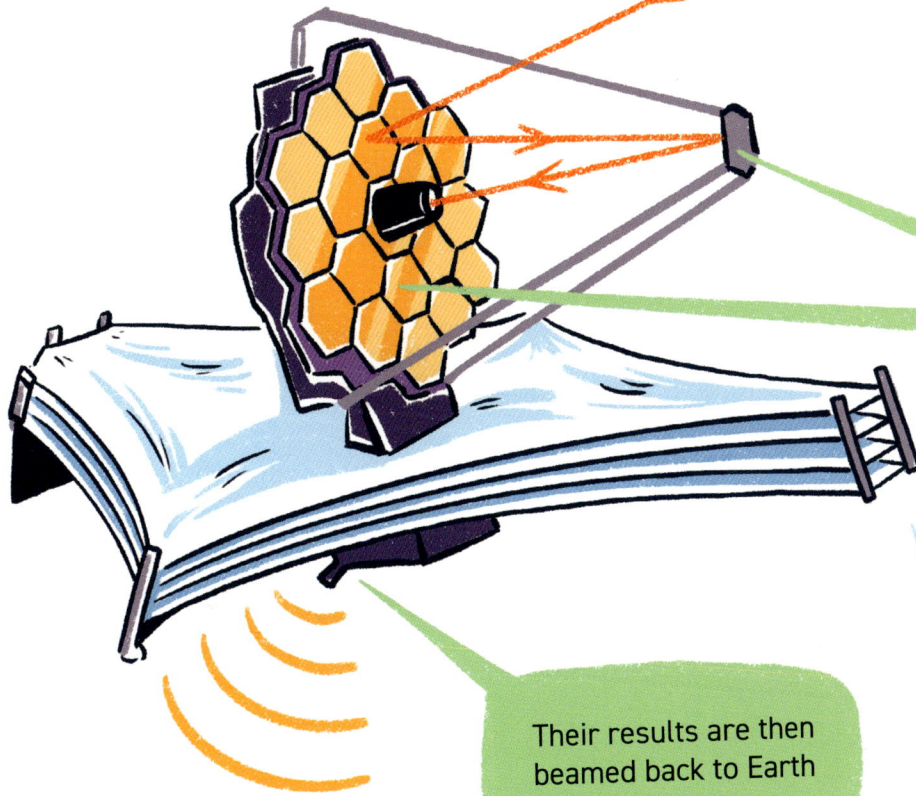

The telescope is powerful enough to spot a football 550 km away!

The telescope's mirrors reflect light onto its cameras and other scientific instruments.

Their results are then beamed back to Earth by a radio antenna.

The shield is about the size of a tennis court. That's a BIG sun shade!

To keep the telescope's electronics super-cool, a five-layer shield protects the telescope from the Sun's glare. It also houses solar panels which create electricity to power the telescope.

Wow!

PROBING AWAY

JUNO

After a five-year journey, this solar-powered probe reached Jupiter in 2016. It has been orbiting the solar system's biggest planet ever since. The probe's science instruments are studying the planet's atmosphere in detail and have discovered many giant storms. Juno's mission will end in 2025, when it crashes into the planet.

Not a sunny day on Jupiter today ...

COMET INTERCEPTOR

This joint European and Japanese mission will hover in space for up to three years waiting for a comet to race by. It will then fly alongside and release two smaller probes to get up close and personal and measure the chemicals the comet contains.

Wait for me!

LUCY

Lucy blasted off in 2021, powered by two large fold-out parasols covered in solar panels. Lucy has quite a journey ahead, flying to eight asteroids over 12 years. It will deploy instruments at each asteroid to measure what materials they contain. This data may provide clues about how the solar system formed.

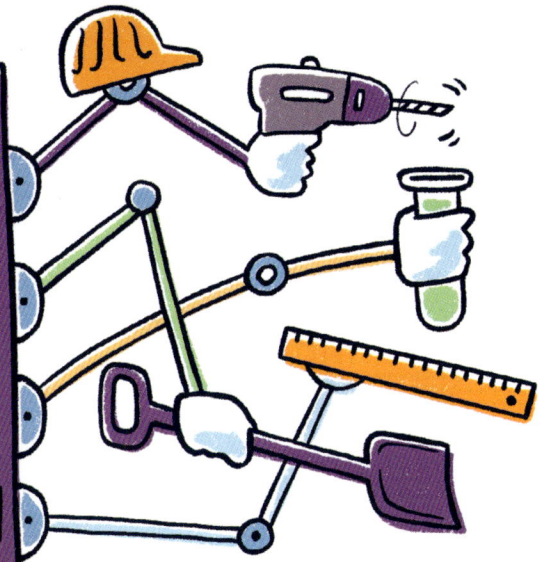

Yippee, I'm going home!

MARS SAMPLE RETURN

Space scientists would love to get their hands on some fresh samples of Mars' surface. This ambitious probe may fulfil their dreams in the 2020s. It would land on Mars, gather key rocks and soil, and load them up into canisters aboard a smaller probe, which would then blast off back to Earth.

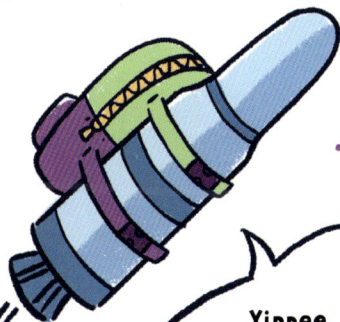

A CLOSER LOOK AT:
THE PARKER SOLAR PROBE

This is the first probe to actually touch the Sun (well, its outer atmosphere) and survive! The Parker Solar Probe is making 24 swooping orbits around the Sun, each time getting closer to our fiery star as it studies its features and the energy and magnetism it produces.

The probe flies by Venus to use that planet's force of gravity to slow itself down and change its orbit angle. This allows it to travel closer to the Sun. In total, the probe will make seven fly-bys of Venus.

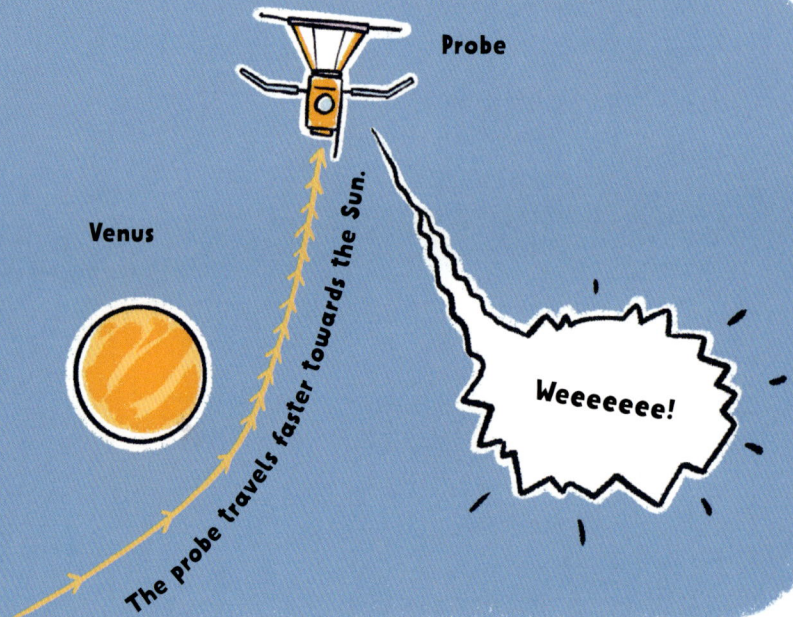

Probe

Venus

The probe travels faster towards the Sun.

Weeeeeee!

Along with a cooling system, the 11.5-cm-thick heat shield protects the probe's delicate instruments from extreme heat. It does a great job – the Sun can heat the outside of the shield to a scorching 1,370 °C, yet inside the probe the temperature is just 30 °C.

Sensors struck by direct sunlight alert the probe's central computer. It fires its small jet thrusters to turn a little so that it keeps the shield squarely facing the Sun and blocking out its heat.

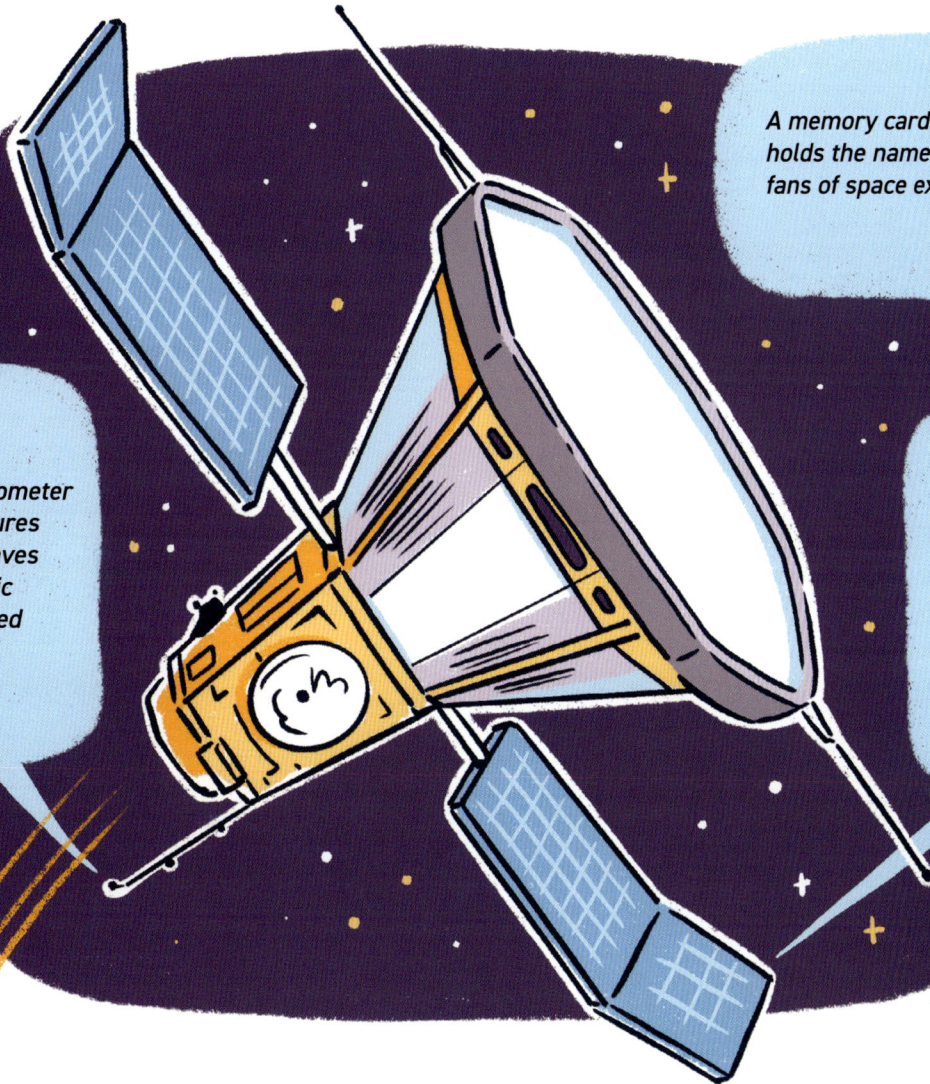

A memory card inside the probe holds the names of 1.1 million fans of space exploration.

The magnetometer boom measures the radio waves and magnetic field produced by the Sun.

Solar panels fold up when too close to the Sun, but fold out farther away to generate electricity.

Earth

Venus

Sun

On each orbit around the Sun, the Parker Solar Probe will circle closer and the Sun's gravity will pull it along faster until it becomes the fastest ever human-made object!

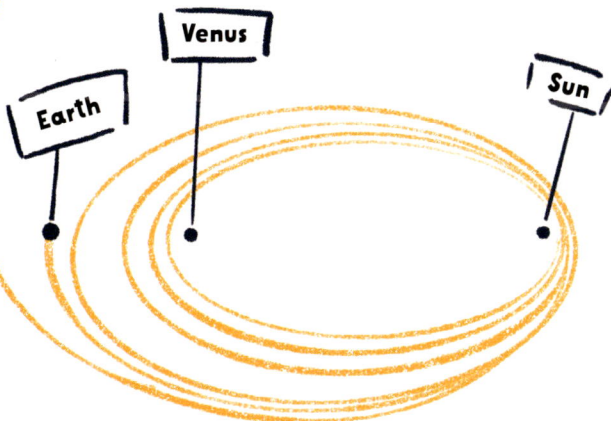

The final orbits in 2025 are expected to see the probe reach speeds of 700,000 km/h – enough to whizz between London and New York and back in under 60 seconds!

ROVING AROUND

PERSEVERANCE

The size of a small car, this six-wheeled Mars rover is packed with science tech including a laser that blasts rock into gas so that other instruments can analyse its contents. Perseverance's MOXIE experiment is trying to make life-giving oxygen out of Mars' atmosphere, which is 95% carbon dioxide.

Kapow!

DRAGONFLY

Launching in 2027, this flying robot will spin its eight one-metre-long rotor blades to hover and fly across Titan – Saturn's largest moon. During 32 months on Titan, it will search for water and chemicals essential for life and study Titan's cryovolcanoes which erupt ice rather than red-hot runny rock.

TUMBLEWEED ROVERS

Large balls made of a light frame covered in tough fabric may explore other worlds in the future. These machines will roll when the wind blows, just like tumbleweed bushes. Inside, scientific instruments can gather data as the ball explores far greater distances than slow-moving wheeled rovers.

MINERVA-II

These hexagonal robots from Japan were carried aboard the Hayabusa2 space probe to an asteroid called Ryugu. Powered by a small, spinning motor, the robots moved by hopping into the air as they explored the asteroid, landing safely on sets of tiny legs.

A CLOSER LOOK AT:
SHAPESHIFTERS

Sending spacecraft to the outer planets like Jupiter and Saturn takes a lot of time and money, so the craft you send need to be capable of doing as many jobs and tasks as possible. NASA are developing a fleet of robot probes that can work together to explore Titan and other moons of Saturn in different ways.

This Shapeshifter's sensors are measuring the ground temperature.

A squadron of Shapeshifters fly low over Titan. Each has different sensors which measure the landscape. Together, the data they collect builds up a complete picture of Titan's surface.

Each Shapeshifter has its own power system with thrusters and propellers. These could be used like helicopter rotor blades to hover in mid-air or to whizz them above ground as they explore.

Shapeshifters are cobots – robots that cooperate with each other. To explore on land, they may lock together so that their curved panels form a ball. This shape allows them to roll across the ground easily as their sensors investigate Titan close-up.

Certain Shapeshifters' propellers spin to drive the ball in a particular direction.

Robots sensors work together to plot the best route to their target.

Titan contains seas made of liquid methane which the probes would investigate. They may form floating rafts on the surface or form sleek, torpedo-shaped craft that can dive down to explore.

LIVING IN SPACE

ASTROBEES

These cute cube-shaped robots use spinning electric fans to fly round a space station, helping astronauts out. A robotic gripper lets them hold onto straps and struts as they video tasks for astronauts and give spoken instructions. They can also act as an extra hand when maintenance tasks are performed.

ASTRO GARDEN

Astronauts may eat more fresh fruit and veg in the future by growing their own in space. Astro Garden is a vertical greenhouse system that grows plants without soil. It recycles water and nutrients and uses computer-controlled LED lighting to mimic sunlight.

I'm a space-grown carrot, I am!

Well, aren't you fancy!

ERA SPACEWALKER

A brand new robot arm was tested on the International Space Station in 2022. The arm is 11.3 m long with a strong grabbing hand at each end. This allows it to grip and release the outside of the craft and move the rest of its arm to walk freely along the spacecraft's exterior.

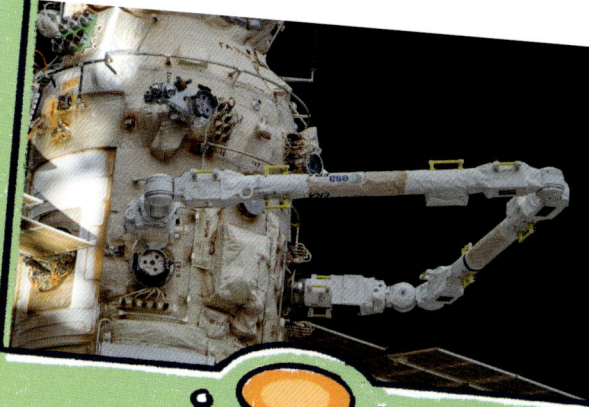

RHEALTH ONE

rHealth One is a doctor in a box that uses two tiny lasers to analyse small samples of astronauts' blood, saliva or wee. It can diagnose medical conditions that may affect astronauts in space, such as bone loss, exposure to radiation or heart disease, and beam the details back to doctors on Earth.

Not wee again! I always get the wee ...

It's a spit day for me today!

A CLOSER LOOK AT:
SPACESUITS

Spacesuits have stayed the same for the past 40 years but that's all set to change. The challenges of sending astronauts to the Moon, and possibly Mars in the future, mean super tech suits, like NASA's xEMU, are being developed for future missions.

When it's time to suit up, an astronaut will climb a set of steps and enter the xEMU suit from a hatch at the back. The new suit is less bulky and more flexible than previous models.

Previous suits came in two parts and could take an hour to put on.

The xEMU suit contains joints that allow the astronaut to kneel, reach across their body and raise their arms well above their heads.

The suit is made from more than a dozen layers of different materials. It protects against micrometeoroids – tiny particles that whizz through space so fast they could tear through regular fabrics.

The PLSS backpack is an astronaut's lifesaver. It provides power, water and oxygen and carries away carbon dioxide breathed out by the astronaut. The xEMU suit can support an astronaut in space for up to six days.

The helmet contains radio microphones and speakers so astronauts can stay in touch. It also has a voice-activated video camera and a built-in water pouch and straw.

The visor is coated with a thin layer of pure gold to repel the Sun's rays.

Astronauts will still wear a Maximum Absorbency Garment underneath their high-tech suit. This is an adult nappy!

Each glove fingertip contains a microheater to keep fingers warm in the bitter cold of space.

Boots with soft soles are used for clambering around the exterior of a spacecraft on a spacewalk. Sturdier, hard-soled boots would be used for walking on the Moon or Mars.

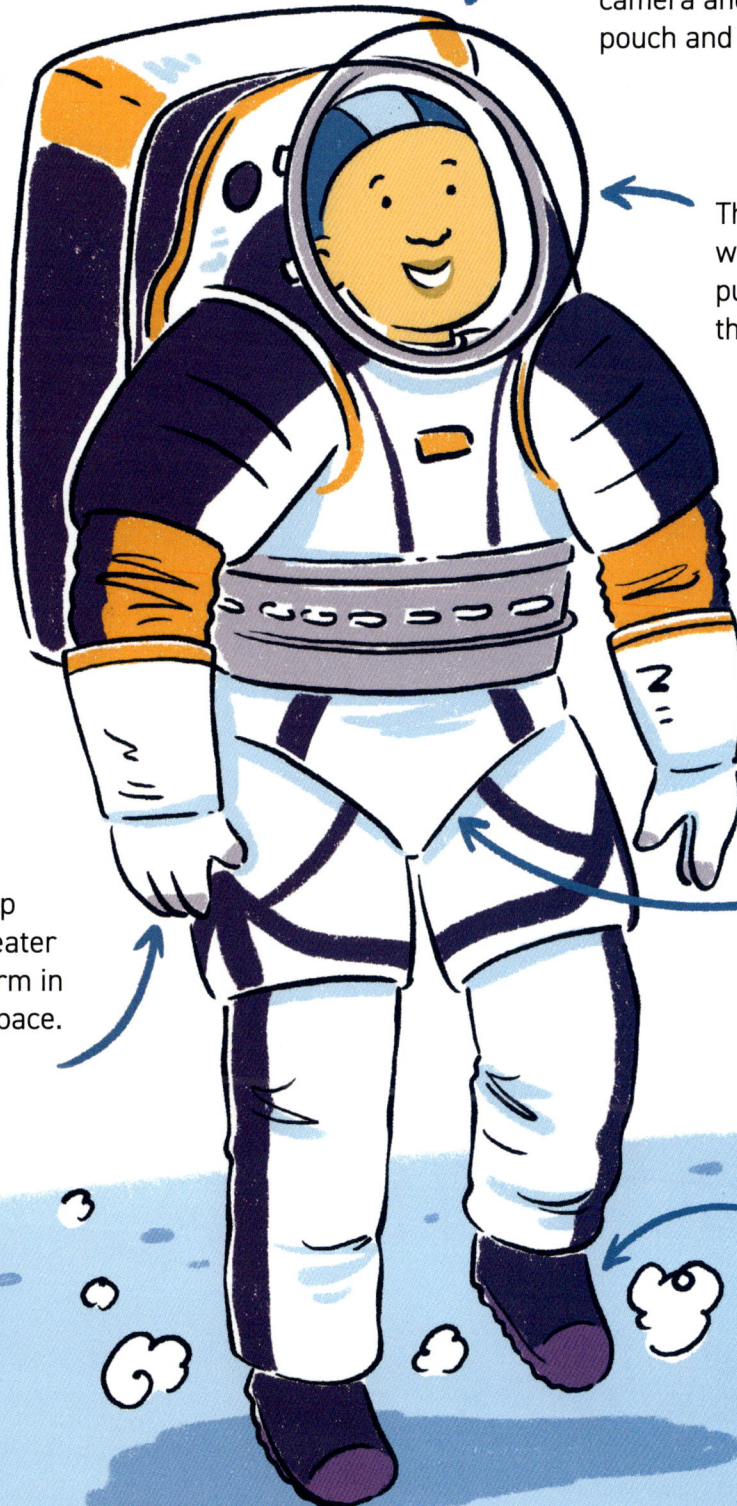

FUTURE VOYAGES

ARTEMIS

The last astronaut stood on the Moon in 1972. NASA thinks it's high time, humans returned. Artemis will place a space station into orbit around the Moon and a base camp on the lunar surface near its south pole. Astronauts will travel between the two in a lunar lander craft.

It's hard work to inflate a space module!

STARLAB

This future space station will house four astronauts inside an inflatable module. This would be packed flat in a rocket during launch to save space. Once in space, it would be inflated with air to form a large, pressurised area for the astronauts to live and work in.

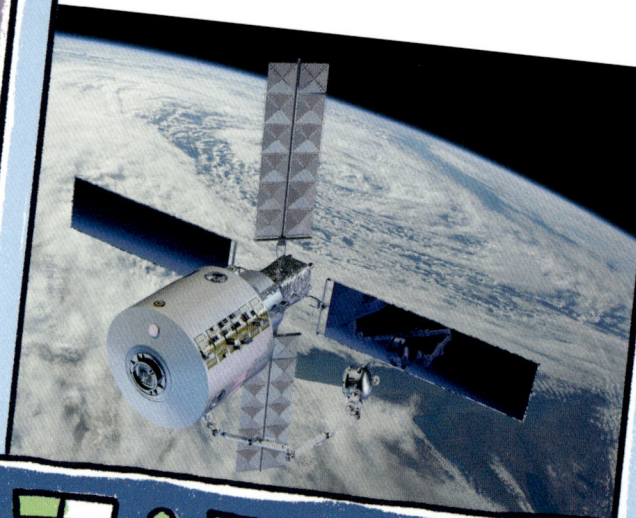

Just popping down to the Moon to pick up some milk.

NEW SHEPARD

Named after Alan Shepard, the first American in space, this rocket-powered capsule carries six space tourists on a thrilling voyage into near space. The craft takes off and lands vertically, aided by drag brakes and parachutes to slow it down on its descent.

Mum, are we there yet?

ORBITAL REEF

This ambitious space station will be a hotel for out-of-this-world holidays 500 km above Earth. Large windows in the interconnecting pods that make up the station will give incredible views for ten lucky people. The station will also house medical and materials research and other science projects.

A CLOSER LOOK AT:
A FUTURE MARS BASE

It's the dream of many space scientists – a human colony on Mars, tens of millions of kilometres from Earth. Space tech would be needed to solve many problems living on a cold planet with no native plants, oxygen or surface water.

The voyage to Mars would take at least six to 18 months and parts of the base may be built in advance by robots sent on unmanned missions. Regular cargo spacecraft would bring supplies and materials from Earth as the base develops.

Inflatable domes filled with plants would provide fresh food to the colonists. Oxygen would be processed from Mars' carbon dioxide-rich atmosphere. Water may be extracted from ice found underground or carried from the planet's polar ice caps.

Mobile robots could keep the panels clean after frequent Martian dust storms.

Mars is farther away from the Sun than Earth but it has cloudless skies, so giant arrays of solar panels could generate the colony's electricity.

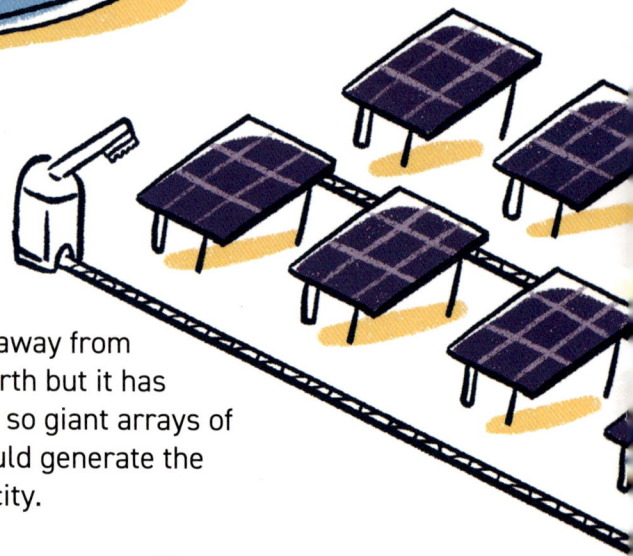

Robots might mine the Martian surface for valuable minerals. Some may be processed into fuel to power spacecraft heading back to Earth.

All-terrain rovers would explore the Martian surface and dock with the base's airlocks.

The average temperature on Mars is a freezing -63 °C, so colonists would need a lot of energy to keep warm. Part of the base may be built underground to insulate it from the cold on the surface.

TECH TEST

1. Where is the Perseverance rover currently exploring?
a) Mars
b) The Moon
c) Jupiter

2. Which flying robot will explore Saturn's moon, Titan?
a) Ingenuity
b) PLATO
c) Dragonfly

3. The MINERVA-II rovers explored what sort of object in space?
a) A comet
b) An asteroid
c) A moon of Jupiter

4. Where is the Extremely Large Telescope being built?
a) Spain
b) Chile
c) Russia

5. Which space probe will reach speeds of 700,000 km/h on its mission?
a) Comet Interceptor
b) Juno
c) Parker Solar Probe

6. How many tonnes of fuel do the SLS's booster rockets use up per second?
a) 0.6 tonnes
b) 6 tonnes
c) 60 tonnes

7. Which space probe will visit and investigate eight asteroids during its 12 year mission?
a) Lucy
b) FAST
c) Astrobees

8. Which rocket-powered vehicle launched the James Webb Space Telescope?
a) Space Ship III
b) Falcon Heavy
c) Ariane 6

EXPLORE MORE
GLOSSARY

antenna A dish or rod on a spacecraft used to transmit and receive radio signals.

asteroid An irregular rocky object, smaller than a planet, orbiting the Sun.

atmosphere The layers of gas that surround a planet, held in place by the planet's gravity.

comet A small, icy body that orbits the Sun. When it gets close to the Sun, heat causes it to lose gas and dust which forms a long tail.

exoplanet A planet found outside of the solar system.

galaxy A vast collection of millions of stars, planets, gas, and dust bound together by gravity.

gravity The invisible force of attraction between objects.

radiation Energy, such as infrared, X-rays and visible light, that travels through space in waves.

orbit To circle around another object, for example when a moon orbits around a planet.

thruster Rocket engines used for manoeuvring a machine in space.

FURTHER INFORMATION

BOOKS

Code STEM: Space Tech – Max Wainewright & John Haslam (Wayland, 2020)

Out Of This World Space Tech – Clive Gifford (Wayland, 2020)

The Cosmic Diary of our Incredible Universe – Tim Peake (Wren & Rook, 2022)

ON THE WEB

www.nasa.gov/topics/technology/
The website of the US space agency NASA is packed with news, photos and videos of their latest spacecraft and technology.

www.rocketstem.org
A brilliant website packed with news, features and quizzes for budding young space engineers and explorers.

www.rmg.co.uk/stories/topics/nasa-moon-mission-artemis-program-launch-date
Learn lots of fascinating facts and watch stunning videos about plans to send human astronauts back to the Moon at this website from Royal Museums Greenwich.

www.youtube.com/watch?v=Lti6a_YYQl0
This entertaining video explains how rocket engines work to blast off from Earth and head into space.

Every effort has been made by the Publishers to ensure that the websites in this book are suitable for children, that they are of the highest educational value, and that they contain no inappropriate or offensive material. However, because of the nature of the Internet, it is impossible to guarantee that the contents of these sites will not be altered. We strongly advise that internet access is supervised by a responsible adult.

INDEX

Answers
1a, 2c, 3b, 4b, 5c, 6b, 7a, 8c.